Jesus Paid It All "True Hero"

HEROES OF FAITH

Elder Steve Carter, Jr.

Foreword

He is a Leader, Preacher, Teacher and a great example.

Elder Steve Carter, Jr. is an exceptional man that exemplifies what it is to live a purpose driven life. He continues to take steps higher to accomplishing his goals and deepening his relationship with God. He strives to be very proactive in living out all that he was created to do.

Mr. Carter has such an admirable ability to receive and digest the gospel, teach and then apply valuable information. His obstacles do not keep him down. Instead, they are transformed into tools that contribute to his further growth and development.

In different ways, Mr. Carter has inspired me over the last few months to experience transformation in my own life. I am a better person for having crossed paths with him, and I've often thought of him with gratitude for the way his friendship has impacted my life.

~ J. Carol Grant

Introduction

This is a walk through the trying of your faith that will build your faith and will encourage your heart to hold on to God's unchanging hand. This mission is also a trying of your faith as you go on life's journey in faith towards God. God will give you the victory every time, because we are more than conquerors in Christ Jesus. As you travel through life's journey, you will find out that all of God's words are true.

The Book of Job is a good book to study. The trying of Job's faith will help build your faith to hold on to your unchanging hope, which is in Christ Jesus, the hope of Glory. We must believe God's word because he is a God that will not lie. To receive God's promise we must obey his word and scriptures as it is written. Amen.

The Gospel must be preached among all nations. For God so loved the world that he gave his only begotten son, that whosoever believeth in him should not perish, but have everlasting life. The purpose of this book is that you may understand more about our Lord and Savior, and to build your faith even more in the glorious gospel of Jesus Christ our Lord. God is a spirit, and those that worship him, must also worship him in spirit and truth. When Jesus was born, died, buried, and rose from the dead, hope was resurrected.

Written by Elder Steve Carter, Jr.

TABLE OF CONTENTS

Chapter 1: Heroes of Faith

To become a hero of faith, we must come to God believing that he will reward those who diligently seek HIM. Now take a walk with me into God's Hall of Fame of Faith and you will get a glimpse of the power of faith when people get involved in an active partnership with God, and the power of following the principle of faith according to what is written.

"But the just shall live by faith." When we look at the greatest men of faith in the word of God, such as Abel, Enoch, Noah, Abraham, Isaac, Jacob, Joseph and Moses, these men are members of an exclusive fraternity for our teaching.

Hebrew 11:4 gives us a picture of true faith when Abel offered unto God a more excellent sacrifice than Cain by which he obtained witness that he was righteous. God testifying of his gifts and by it he being dead yet speaketh.

When Adam and his wife sinned against God, Genesis 3:21 tells us that unto Adam and his wife, did the Lord God make coats of skins and clothe them. God was the first one to make the first sacrifice; blood was shed. This is where the priest who would offer up sacrifices for the people's sins came from. But now, Jesus is our peace offering to God our Father. "In the beginning was the word; and the word was with God; and the word was God."

Chapter 2: God's Word Transforms

All things were made by him, and the word was made flesh and dwelt among us and we beheld his glory. The glory of the only begotten of the Father, full of grace and truth. The miracles from Genesis to Revelation, which is written in the Bible, are the miracles of Jesus. Jesus is and always has been a miracle worker.

He came to transform us in the likeness of himself. The word of God includes the scriptures of the Old Testament as well as the New Testament. One is not without the other. By faith, Enoch was taken away so that he did not see death, and was not found because God had taken him. For before he was taken, he had this testimony that he pleased God. Hebrews 11:5.

So all the days of Enoch were 365 years Genesis 5:23. By faith, Noah being divinely warned of things not yet seen, moved with Godly fear and prepared an ark for the saving of his household. By which he condemned the world and became heir of the righteousness which is according to faith. Hebrews 11:7.

By faith Abraham obeyed when he was called to go out to the place which he would receive as an inheritance. And he went out not knowing where he was going. By faith, Abraham when he was tested offered up Isaac his only son after he received promises from God. In Isaac your seed shall be called. Hebrews 11:17-18.

By faith, Jacob saw things concerning things to come by faith. Jacob when he was dying blessed each of the sons of Joseph and worshipped leaning on the top of his staff Hebrews 11:21. What person can be compared with God enthroned on high? For below him are the heavens and earth.

He stopped to look your kindness and love are as vast as the vast heavens. Your faithfulness is higher than the skies. Moses by faith, he forsook Egypt not fearing the wrath of the king for endured as seeing him who is invisible.

Chapter 3: Temptation and Suffering

Let no man say when he is tempted. Say I am tempted of God for God cannot be tempted with evil, neither tempt he any man.

But he will allow us to be tested and will make a way for us to escape temptation. For whosoever shall keep the whole low and yet offend in one point he is guilty of all. For he that said do not commit adultery said also do not kill. We cannot do away with the word of God; his commandment. Paul tells us in Colossians 1:23-25.

Paul is showing us how now he rejoices in his sufferings for us and filled up that which is behind of the affliction of Christ in his flesh for the body of Christ's sake which is the church that he might fulfill the word of God.

My friend it is not enough to just say "Lord I believe" and not follow the instruction he gives us in the word of God and still expect good results. God has given us the Bible, we are to live every word that comes from God's word. Because in the beginning God's word was and it became flesh. In Christ Jesus was the fullness of God. God has given us a perfect way to live on this earth.

Remember we all have a choice to serve sin or to serve righteous living. When you look at the Heroes of Faith in your Bible, they teach us how to stand firm in faith. We read about the miracle that Jesus did. They were done by him that we might believe. He was sent from God the Father. When Nicodemus came to Jesus by night and asked Jesus, Jesus told him he must be born again. "Are though a master of Israel and know not these things?"

Verily, verily I say unto thee, we speak that we do know and testify that we have seen and ye receive not our witness St. John 3:9-10. St. John 3:16 For God so loved the world that he gave his only begotten son. That whosoever believeth in him should not perish, but have everlasting life. St. John 2:11 tells us the beginning of miracles Jesus did in Cannon of Galilee and manifested forth is Glory and his disciples believed in him.

For Jesus tells us in Mathews 4:4, it was written man shall not live by bread alone, but every word that proceeded out of the mouth of God. Jesus came to bless our soul and spirit. Matthew 5:3 tells us that blessed are the poor in spirit for theirs is the kingdom of heaven. Matthew 8:26 Jesus said unto them why are ye fearful. O ye of little faith? Our faith has to be tried in the fire to see if we are able to stand Satan.

St. John 14:1 Jesus tells us let not our hearts be troubled. If we believe in God, believe also in Him. In my Father's house there are many mansions. If it were not so, I would have told you. I go to prepare a place for you. And if I go and prepare a place for you, I will come again and receive you unto myself. That where I am, there ye may be also. And whether I go, ye know and the way ye know.

He that hath my commandments and keep them, it is he that loveth me and be loved of my father also. And I will love him and will manifest myself to him. John 14:1-4. John 14:21. I am the true vine and my Father is the husbandman. Every branch that bareth fruit, he pergeth it that it may bring forth more fruit.

As we know the fruit we are to bring forth, it is the rightness of God of good works. If we truly have faith, we must put our faith to the test, to see if we have the faith of our Lord. Matthew 12:37-39. For by the words thou shall be justified and by thy word oh Lord, we shall be condemned.

Then certain of the scribes and Pharisees answered saying "Master we would see a sign." And Jesus said "there shall no sign be given to it, but the sign of the prophet Jonah. As Jonah was in the belly of the whale, so shall the son of man be in the heart of the earth three days and three nights. God is speaking the same words he spoke in the beginning. He changes not. Amen.

Chapter 4: He Is God

Revelation 1:8 tells us that Jesus Christ is Alpha and Omega; the beginning and the ending. The first and the last. Which is and which was, and which is to come. The Almighty. I feel sorry for the people today who do not believe that Jesus still performs miracles at the hands of Jesus because the miracle of the new birth is the greatest miracle of all.

Put your hope in the Lord your God because with the Lord, there is grace and mercy, and with him there is unlimited forgiveness. Do not let circumstances change the way you see Jesus. Let Jesus change the way you see circumstances. Because he was wounded for our transgressions, he was bruised for our inequities and the chastisement of our peace was upon Him and by his stripes we are healed: Isaiah 55:5.

St. John 3:16 lets us know that God so loved the world that he gave his only begotten son. That whosoever believeth in him should not perish, but have everlasting life. Do you believe that Jesus died on the cross for your sins? Have you made Him Lord over your life? Do you keep his word? Because He says: "If you love me, keep my commandments."

Jesus Paid It All

Chapter 5: He Paid It All

Jesus came to this earth and paid for our sins. The debt that God our heavenly father required for the wages of sin. Jesus paid for our salvation when he laid down his life on the cross. It was for our physical body and for our soul. And he will supply all of our needs according to his riches in glory by Christ Jesus. Philippians 4:19.

Jesus came to give us spiritual life because our life is hidden within him. And this is the faith and hope that we have in Christ Jesus. And we are to be faithful to the word of God until the end. He tells us in Luke 16:12; If ye have not been faithful in that which is another man, who shall give you that which is your own?

No servant can serve two masters for either he will hate the one and love the other or else he will hold to the one and despise the other. We cannot serve God and man. When we follow not God's instructions given to us in his word, we may delay the blessings God has for us. These great men of faith traded their doubts and unbelief for faith. They believed in God.

There is no greater Love than he showed us when He laid down His life for us. He calls us his friends should we continue in sin that his grace may abound upon us. No God forbid. Let us not crucify him afresh.

My dear friend unbelief and doubt and fear closes the door to God's blessings. But faith opens the door to God's truth and promises. Jeremiah 31:33 God says "I will write my laws upon their hearts and minds. I will be their God and they shall be my people. St. John 15:7 says it will be given to you and Jesus spoke a parable unto them to this end. That men ought to always pray and not give up Luke 18:1.

We can always trust God. He says he will never leave us nor forsake us. Now faith is the assurance of things we hope for. The certainty of things that we cannot see.

When the apostles was preaching the gospel of Christ, their theme was Christ's death and he was raised from the dead. And they were eye witness. Christ the miracle worker in his humiliation in his purity and holiness in his matchless love was to be their theme. And in order not only as received in his life and teaching but as foretold by the prophets of the Old Testaments and as symbolized by the sacrificial service.

Christ died for us when we were yet sinners, then hope was born. A new life in Christ but it is by your own choice. Are you being led by God or just following the crowd? For as many are led by the spirit of God, they are the sons of God Romans 8:14. When Jesus came walking on the water and Peter said "If it be you Lord, bid me to come." Jesus said "Come." When we are tried and tested in our faith, will we hold on to our faith or will we let go as Peter did and began to sink.

But holding on to our faith in God and our Lord and Savior, Jesus Christ tells us in St. John 14:1 let not your heart be troubled, ye who believe in God also believe in me. Job 1:6 now there was a day when the sons of God came to present themselves before the Lord and Satan came also.

Chapter 6: The Tempter

And the Lord said unto Satan, "Where goeth thou?" Then Satan answered the Lord and said, "From going to and fro in the earth and from walking up and down in it, seeking whom I can devour." And the Lord asked him, "Has thou considered my servant Job. There is none like him in the earth; a perfect and upright man. One that fears God and eschewed evil."

And Satan said, "Doth Job fear God naught? Has not thou made a hedge about him and about his house, and about all that he hath on every side? Thou hast blessed the work of his hands and his substance is increased in the land. But put forth your hand now and touch all that he hath and he will curse thee to thy face." And the Lord said unto Satan, "Behold all that he hath is in thy power only upon himself put not forth thine hand." We all know the story how Job lost all that he had. This was the first time Satan attacked Job. But he held to his integrity. But if we keep reading we will see where Satan was given another chance when he touched Job's body with sickness, but Job still held onto God's hand.

Has God chosen you to be one of his champions of faith? James 1:2 My brethren, count it all joy when ye fall into diver's temptations knowing this, that the trying of your faith worketh patience, but let patience have her perfect work that ye may be perfect wanting nothing. If any of us lack wisdom, let us ask God that giveth to all men liberally.

But let him as in faith, not wavering. So let us therefore come boldly to the throne of grace and find grace in time of need, because without the shedding of blood, there is no forgiveness of sin. The laws of the Lord are right and those who obey them are happy. The commands of the Lord are just and give understanding to the mind Psalms 19:8.

Faith comes by hearing and hearing by the word of God. Romans 10:17 the power of knowing God's truth and the truth shall make us free. St. John 1:1 In the beginning was the word and the word was God and the word was with God.

The same was in the beginning with God. All things were made by him and without him was not anything made that was made. In Him was life and the life was the light of men. And the light shineth in darkness and the darkness comprehended it not. St. John 1:11. He came unto his own. His own received him not.

We know when the tempter came to Jesus tempting him after he has fasted 40 days and 40 nights. Satan knew that Jesus was hungry, so Satan came to Jesus in his weakest hour, but Jesus was not going to obey Satan. It is the way of the cross. Through the things we go through, when we can go through and not yield to sin, this is the victory we have in Jesus. True faith is knowing that Jesus will never leave us nor forsake us.

Jesus says I am the way, the truth, and the life. No man cometh unto the Father but by me. God the Father, God the Son, and the Holy Ghost are the same God. They are one. The word of God became flesh because in Him was the fullness of the God head body, and we beheld his glory. The glory as of the only begotten of the Father; full of grace and truth.

Chapter 7: The Finisher of Our Faith

Jesus is the author and finisher of our faith. And through His death and resurrection from the dead there is salvation. We know as believers, Jesus, the son of God, laid down His life on the cross for our sins. It is only through His blood He shed on the cross for our sins. He was the lamb that was slain for the foundation of the world. And true faith is following God's instruction. Jesus told Simon Peter to launch out into the deep and let down his net for a catch. But Simon answered and said "Master we have toiled all night and caught nothing. Nevertheless at you word I will do it."

And when he obeyed Jesus' words they caught a great number of fish. As we look at Peter's obedience to Jesus' words, he was blessed through his faith. Take a moment and read this faith building story from your Bible that tells what Jesus said and did. So faith cometh by hearing and hearing by the word of God. He is King of King and Lord of Lord. Pilate therefore said unto Jesus, "Art thou a King then?" Jesus answered, "Thou sayest that I am a king and for this cause came into the world that I should bear witness unto the truth."

The Book of Acts 26:18 when Saul was struck down and was blinded, he was given instructions what he was to do. Jesus had a plan for his life. To send him to the Gentiles as a witness. To open their eyes and to turn them from darkness to light. And for an inheritance among them which are sanctified by faith that is in Christ Jesus.

If you refuse to do your part, you cut yourself off from God's part. I pray that you will do your part so God can do his part because God's spirit will not always strive with man.

Wherefore as the Holy Ghost say today if ye hear my voice harden not your heart Hebrews 3:7-8. Put your hope in the Lord because with the Lord there is mercy and grace and unlimited forgiveness. Paul tells us in Romans 6:1-2 what shall we say then? Shall we continue to sin that eternal grace may abound? God forbid. Romans 6:23 For the wage of sin is death but the gift of God is eternal life through Jesus Christ our Lord. Jesus was the gift God gave. His only begotten son, so we must not let sin rule over us. Romans 6:12 tells us let not sin therefore reign in your mortal body that ye should obey it in the lust thereof. I thank God and my Lord and Savior Jesus Christ for his grace and mercy.

He loved me so much that he laid down His life on the cross for man's sin. He paid our sin debt once and for all, but man was created with freedom of choice. God was going to destroy man whom he had created from the face of the earth. Both man and beast and the creeping things, and the fowls of the air, for it repententh me that I have made them.

But Noah Found grace in the eyes of the Lord. Now knowing therefore being justified by faith, we have peace with God through our Lord Jesus Christ, by whom we also have access by faith into His grace wherein we stand. And rejoice in hope of tribulations of the trying of our faith. We must have glory in tribulation also knowing that tribulations work patience, and patience, experience, experience, hope. And hope make not ashamed because the love of God is shed abroad in our hearts by the Holy Ghost which is given unto us.

And when we were yet without strength in due time Christ died for the ungodly, but God commended his love toward us in that while we were yet sinners, Christ died for us.

Chapter 8: His Grace

John 1:16 And of His fullness all have received grace. For the law was given by Moses, but grace and truth came by Jesus Christ. We must learn to live by God's word in obedience to Him through faith in Him. God is still speaking to us through his word. The Bible is the written word of God.

As we live by God's word through faith that God has forgiven us of our sins past, present, and future, we must turn from our sins and live by God's standard. When we accept Jesus as our Lord and savior we must take off the old man and put on the new man. We must take up righteousness and put on the righteousness of God. Just because we are not under the law, should we continue to sin, God forbid.

Colossians 2:13 and you being dead in your sins and the uncircumcised of your flesh has he quickened together with him having forgiven us all trespasses. Blotting out the hand writing ordinances that was against us which was contrary to us and took it out the way nailing it to His cross. Amen.

It is the way of the cross Jesus said. If any man will come after him, let him first deny himself and take up his cross and follow him. When Jesus was nailed to the cross, he paid our sin debt in full. And now in his death, burial, and resurrection, I am to walk in newness of life which is rightness. Always abounding in all truth. When Christ died, I died with Him. When I accepted Him as my Lord and Savior in baptism, I was buried with Christ and when He rose, I rose. I rose from the dead through faith. Through His grace and mercy I am saved.

God grace and mercy does not give me the right to continue sinning. Revelation 22:12 and behold I come quickly and my reward is with me to give to every man according as his work shall be. I am Alpha and Omega. The beginning and the end. The first and the last. Blessed are they that do His commandments, that they may have right to the tree of life, and may enter in through the gates into the city.

For without are dogs, and sorcerers, and whoremongers, and idolaters, and whosever loveth and maketh a lie. I Jesus have sent mine angel to testify unto you these things in the churches. For I testify unto every man that heareth the words of the prophecy of this book. If any man shall add unto these things, God shall add unto him the plagues that are written in this book.

And if any man shall take away from the words of the book of this prophecy, God shall take away his part out of the book of life, and out of the Holy city, and from the things which are written in this book, which is the Bible. How can we say that we believe in God and His son Jesus, but we believe His word through faith, the Bible.

Jesus says I did not come to condemn the world, but that the world might be saved through him. But if we don't believe that Jesus died on the cross and shed his blood for your sins, we are already condemned. We are spherical dead because the life is in the blood and in Christ who is our life appear then shall we also appear with him in glory, and the scriptures cannot be broken. It has been established in heaven by God.

Chapter 9: Give Up Your Life For Christ

We are to give up our life for Christ's life. He gave His life for us while we were yet sinners. He died for us. Colossians 3:6 Let the word of Christ dwell in you richly. In all wisdom teaching and admonishing one another in psalms and hymns and spiritual songs singing with grace in your hearts to the Lord. Faith without works is dead. We cannot have faith without works. They work together.

Paul tells us I count not myself to have apprehended nothing, but one thing I do forgetting those things which are behind and reaching forth unto those thing which are before pressing toward the mark for the prize of the high calling of God in Christ Jesus. I thank God for His truth. Malachi 3:6 for I am the Lord. I change not. His word stays the same forever more. Amen.

We are washed through his word. James 1:23 for if any be a hearer of the word and not a doer, he is like a man beholding his natural face in a glass. Why do I do the things that I do? It is because of Christ that lives in me and not of myself. He enables me to go through trials and tests. Only through him can I be more than a conqueror. And who or what shall separate me from the love of God.

Romans 1:1-4 Paul a servant of Jesus Christ called to be an Apostle separated unto the Gospel of God. Which he had promised afore by his prophets in the Holy Scripture concerning his son Jesus our Lord. Which was made of the seed of David according to the flesh and declared to be the son of God. With power according to the spirit of holiness by the resurrection of the dead.

Do you believe that Jesus died for your sins? Do you believe he was buried and rose from the dead? Do you believe that the blood he shed on the cross was for your sins? All this was done so that you may have eternal life. Have you received him as your Lord and savior? Do you live by his word in all things?

Romans 16:26 But now is made manifested any by the scriptures of the prophets according to the commandment of the everlasting God, made known to all nations for the obedience of faith. Exodus 19:5 Now therefore if ye will obey my voice indeed and keep my covenant then ye shall be a peculiar treasure unto me above all people for all the earth is the Lord's. When we come to God and pray His will to be done in our lives with confidence knowing that He will hear us, faith cometh by hearing and hearing by the word of God. Jesus is our hero. He knows our past and our future. If we would come to the foot of the cross where Jesus shed His blood for our sins, we will find forgiveness. That is the reason Jesus died on the cross; to forgive us of our sins. He will wash us from our unrighteousness and sanctify us through His word.

Chapter 10: The Teacher

God spoke mouth to mouth with Moses. These are the words which thou shall speak unto the children of Israel. And Moses came and called for the elders of the people and laid before their faces all these words, which the lord commanded him. Paul tells Timothy in 2 Timothy 2:1-2 thou before my son, be strong in the grace that is in Christ Jesus. And the thing that he had heard of him, among many witnesses, the same to commit to faithful men, who shall be able to teach others also. Should we not teach the same things Jesus taught and did?

Teaching the word of God not adding nor taking away from the truth of God's word. The Bible is the true word of God's word. It is our power of knowing the truth. Jesus is our only hope for salvation. Without him we have no hope. It is only in God's only son, Jesus Christ, we are transformed in the newness of life.

When God told Abraham to get from among his people and he would make him a Father of many nations, Abraham obeyed God. He took God at his word and God kept His promise to Abraham. He will do the same for us today. If we are willing to obey His voice. Amen.

God is still talking to us today in His word and the revelation of His word. Once we come to the truth of God's word, and when we are troubled on every side to rest with them. Paul is telling us to rest. And when the Lord Jesus shall be revealed from heaven with His mighty angels in flaming fire, taking vengeance on them that know not God, and that obey not the gospel of our Lord Jesus Christ.

Author Biography

Elder Steve Carter Jr is the son of a Southern Baptist Deacon. All of his life he has been immersed in an environment heavily encouraged by the gospel. He is one of 13 children his parents brought into the world. Four died at an early age. Four boys and five girls lived to reach adulthood. Elder Steve Carter Jr is the youngest of his siblings; born September 13, 1953, two days before his father's birthday. He married at the age of twenty-one and has been happily married since to Mrs. Liza B. Smith Carter. The two have one son, Charles L. Carter, who shares his parent's love of God's word.

2ii

To Inspire. To Ignite

www.freedomink365.com/2ii

www.ingramcontent.com/pod-product-compliance
Lightning Source LLC
Chambersburg PA
CBHW072057040426
42447CB00012BB/3163